EACH DAY AS IT COMES

Morning and Evening Meditations
for Living Through Change

KAREN LEE TURNER

SWOON RIVER PRESS
NASHVILLE

SWOON RIVER PRESS

NASHVILLE

Copyright ©2024 by Karen Lee Turner

All rights reserved. No part of this publication may be reproduced, stored in a retrieval system, or transmitted in any form or by any means (including electronic, photocopy, or recording) without the prior written permission of the publisher. The only exception is brief quotations in reviews of the work.

Cover and interior design: ©2024 Karen Lee Turner

ISBN: 979-8-218-47715-8

Library of Congress Control Number: 2024915737

karenleeturner.com
swoonriverpress.com

for Nevin

CONTENTS

8	OPENING :	The Backstory
14	INVITATION:	How to Use This Book
20	MONDAY:	Clarity & Direction
34	TUESDAY:	Creativity & Delight
48	WEDNESDAY:	Rest & Renewal
62	THURSDAY:	Calling & Courage
76	FRIDAY:	Healing & Wholeness
90	SATURDAY:	Welcome & Hospitality
104	SUNDAY:	Ritual & Celebration
118	CLOSING:	The Unfolding Story
121	ACKNOWLEDGEMENTS	
126	ABOUT THE AUTHOR	

OPENING

THE BACKSTORY

There is a rope connecting
the back door to the barn.

Taut and muscular
weaving its way through
the pasture and along the creek,
over steppingstones and cow piles,
under clotheslines and stars.

So that when the storms rage
and they will
when the blizzards blow
and they will
when the water rises
and it will

You won't get lost.

You hold on.

THE BACKSTORY

We all have our stories of finding our way through change. The milestones we celebrate. The thresholds we cross. The passings we mourn. Vacant chairs that may or may not get filled by someone new at our table. Whether we're emptying our nests or pursuing a new path, our personal novels pulsate with doors that open and chapters that close. Inevitably, the plot thickens.

Let's face it, invited or uninvited, when change sneaks up or barges in, it's not always a welcome visitor. Because change—*even good change*—means loss. And loss rearranges everything. Inside and out.

I know you know this.

So, when we stand on the brink, or hang in limbo it's only natural to reach out for something to hold on to. Something to sustain us as we traverse into the unknown.

Each Day As It Comes was born out of my own need to hold on to something. Something simple and steady. Something lovely and lyrical. Especially when life feels complicated, shaky, discordant, and utterly bewildering.

I come to this project carrying the story of losing my husband to Lewy Body dementia. For a brilliant, creative man who loved living the life of the mind, it was a cruel irony to suffer. Accompanying Nevin to "the end of the trail," as he called it, frequently felt like stumbling in the dark over tangled roots and jagged rocks. A journey both harrowing and holy, we often teetered on that ambiguous precipice of neither *here,* nor *there.* One certainty we held on to was our deep, abiding love. As well as Nevin's enduring, mischievous humor.

In the days and nights since losing my creative partner and favorite poet, I have wandered in an unknown, often dark landscape. Daily life is strange and disorienting. Sleep is elusive. Even grocery shopping is challenging.

During this time, an attentive friend asked, *"What's helping?"*

Such a great question.

My first thoughts:

Relying on the good company of family, friends, and two Maine Coon cats. Soaking in the wisdom of helpers and healers. Cranking up the music and painting just about anything not moving. Walking in nature. Binge-watching British TV shows. And, at the gentle prompting of another thoughtful friend, journaling every morning. A ritual I once engaged in regularly that went by the wayside with moving, caregiving, dying, exhaustion, and, well—*life*.

Turns out this newfound forgotten morning ritual is kind of a lifesaver. As I continue to journal and explore the question, *"what's helping?"* four surprising things have risen to the top:

THE GIFT OF MOMENTS

No matter how arduous or chaotic the journey, there can still be unexpected moments of calm. Moments of beauty and wonder. Moments of hospitality and humor. Like glimmering lights punctuating a darkened landscape, such moments are pure gold.

THE COMFORT OF RITUAL

Change often brings discombobulated days and the looming loneliness of nighttime. A simple, quiet ritual to welcome the morning and ease into the evening feels like being wrapped in a warm quilt.

THE POWER OF "AND"

The natural rhythms of day and night highlight the small, but power-packed word: *AND*. Sure, life is good. It's also awful. All at the same time. Our stories are nuanced. They contain light *and* dark. Gratitude *and* longing. Sorrow *and* relief. Heaviness *and* levity. Generous use of the word *AND* is a reminder that there are lots of ways we can tell our stories.

THE BEAUTY OF "THIN PLACES"

Years ago, when I traveled to the tiny isle of Iona off the western coast of Scotland, I fell in love with the poetic rhythms of the Celtic language. The immediacy of daily experiences woven into the community blessings. The deep connection with nature. The elevation of what they call *thin places:* where the veil between this world and the next is as diaphanous as a dragonfly wing.

Now, I have a new appreciation for such thin places. My experience of the time between living and loving and the last breath is extraordinarily *thin*. I find myself returning to this lyrical language and imagery over and over. It feels like coming home.

A GENTLE, DAILY NUDGE

For many of us, finding our way through change means finding fresh words and new routines. *Each Day As It Comes* offers a gentle, daily nudge to:

- Look for the *gift of moments.*
- Find *comfort and guidance in a simple ritual* that includes gratitude as well as concern for others.
- Embrace the light *and* the darkness.
- Be open to encountering *thin places in everyday life.*
- *Reimagine our language* for the creative source of life, love, and beauty that is within us and around us.

LET'S FIND OUR WAY, TOGETHER

Wherever you are on your journey, I'm ever grateful that you've found your way to these daily meditations. While this book comes from a deeply personal place, I made it for you, too. We're all going through *something.*

It takes creative courage to live in a changing world desperate for meaning, beauty and belonging. My hope is that *Each Day As It Comes* can help illuminate the paths we travel, uplift the stories we carry, and bring us home to our own inner voice and light.

May it be so.

INVITATION

HOW TO USE THIS BOOK

We cannot live in a world
that is not our own,
in a world that is
interpreted for us by others.

An interpreted world is not a home.

Part of the terror is
to take back our own listening,
to use our own voice,
to see our own light.

— HILDEGARD OF BINGEN —

HOW TO USE THIS BOOK

Welcome to *Each Day As It Comes*. Here you'll find a seven-day weekly cycle of meditations for each morning and evening. Because living through change can be challenging and complicated, I have written and designed these meditations to be *simple and brief*, with plenty of room for listening to your own voice.

So, I invite you to find your comfy spot. Pour a cup of something. Light a candle. Grab a journal, if you'd like. Begin wherever you find yourself in the week. Or, whatever calls to you in the moment.

HERE'S WHAT YOU CAN LOOK FORWARD TO:

- A focused theme for each day of the week.
- Inspiring quotes from poetic voices.
- Lovely ways to greet the morning and evening.
- Guided *Thanksgivings*.
- Guided *Entreaties* on behalf of others.
- Journal prompts for each daily theme.
- Encouraging words for facing the day and preparing for the night.

THE DAILY THEMES:

Like signposts on an unknown path, here are the themes I find helpful to keep in front of me. They are daily reminders of what it takes to survive and thrive on this journey. These themes intermingle the rhythms of action and contemplation, and of inner and outer concerns:

MONDAY: Clarity & Direction

TUESDAY: Creativity & Delight

WEDNESDAY: Rest & Renewal

THURSDAY: Courage & Calling

FRIDAY: Healing & Wholeness

SATURDAY: Welcome & Hospitality

SUNDAY: Ritual & Celebration

Let's begin, shall we?

MONDAY

CLARITY & DIRECTION

Monday Morning

It is your road
and yours alone.

Others may walk it with you.

But no one
can walk it for you.

-RUMI-

MONDAY MORNING

QUIET CENTERING

Take a couple of slow, deep breaths.

Enjoy a few moments of quiet to become present to this new day.

GREETING THE DAY

Light above me.
Light within me.
Light on my way.
As the morning mist
melts from the hilltops,
May the fog
clear from my mind.
May the haze
lift from my soul.
May clarity shine forth
this new day.

MONDAY MORNING

THANKSGIVINGS

clarity & direction

Thank Goodness that I have
awakened this day
to the awakening of life itself.

May there be
Something to do.
Something to hope for.
Something to love.

Today, I am especially grateful for...

*As you begin the day give thanks for
what you notice around you
and within you...*

MONDAY MORNING

ENTREATIES

May love kindle a flame
within my heart for:

All who feel lost
and long for direction.

All who are experiencing
the fog of grief.

All who are unable to
see a path forward.

All who are standing at
a fork in the road.

Especially for...

*Name anyone (or situation)
you hold in your heart this day.*

clarity & direction

MONDAY MORNING

QUIET REFLECTION

clarity & direction

- JOURNAL PROMPT -

As I ponder this moment and the day before me...

What areas of my life would benefit from more clarity, direction, and focus?

MONDAY MORNING

GOING FORTH

Blessed be the day before me.
Blessed be the meandering path on which I go.

Even as the clouds of confusion lift,
May I befriend uncertainty and surprise.

As I listen to my life this day,
may I hear the clear call of love:
In each decision I make
In each action I take,
And in each mistake
I make along the way.

May it be so.

Monday Evening

I am out with
lanterns,
looking for
myself.

— EMILY DICKINSON —

MONDAY EVENING

QUIET CENTERING

Take a couple of slow, deep breaths.

*Enjoy a few moments of quiet to
become present to the gifts of the evening.*

GREETING THE EVENING

*Awed by her splendor
stars near the lovely moon
cover their own
bright faces
when she is roundest
and lights earth with
her silver.*

-SAPPHO-

MONDAY EVENING

THANKSGIVINGS

As the day dims, and dusk
gives way to moonlight,

I give thanks for clarity.

For light in the darkness.

For clues and signposts on my path.

For leaps of faith
along the way.

This evening, I am especially grateful for…

Recall the events of the day with gratitude…

clarity & direction

MONDAY EVENING

ENTREATIES

Oh stars in the night sky,
may your shimmering light
shine on me and

All who feel lost.

All who feel alone and confused.

All whose own light
has dimmed.

Especially for…

*Name anyone (or situation)
you hold in your heart this evening.*

clarity & direction

MONDAY EVENING

QUIET REFLECTION

-JOURNAL PROMPT-

*As I take stock of the day,
were there times when I wondered,*

"What now?"

When or where have I found more
clarity, direction, or focus?

clarity & direction

MONDAY EVENING

CLOSING THE EVENING

I surrender to the night
in hopes of a new dawn.

May comfort surround me in the darkness.

May calm ease my monkey mind.

May serenity visit my dreams and
bring the peace of slumber.

This night.
And always.

May it be so.

TUESDAY

CREATIVITY & DELIGHT

Tuesday Morning

Sometimes I've believed as many as six impossible things before breakfast.

– LEWIS CARROLL –

TUESDAY MORNING

QUIET CENTERING

Take a couple of slow, deep breaths.

Enjoy a few moments of quiet to become present to this new day.

GREETING THE DAY

May beauty and wonder
awaken my senses:

Each thing my eyes see.
Each sound I hear.
Each scent I smell.
Each taste I savor.
Each touch that comforts and enlivens.
Each cosmic cause for laughter.

May I pay attention today
and be surprised.

TUESDAY MORNING

THANKSGIVINGS

Thanks be to the Creative Spirit
within me and around me that
I have awakened this day to
the awakening of life itself.

For the color-filled world,
For bright ideas from
unexpected places,
For creative voices that
challenge and uplift me,
For belly-laughs that
sneak up on me,

I give thanks.

Today, I am especially grateful for...

*As you begin the day give thanks for
what you notice around you and within you.*

creativity & delight

TUESDAY MORNING

ENTREATIES

May love kindle a flame
within my heart for:

All who have lost
a sense of humor and wonder.

All who endeavor to see
beauty and connection.

All who struggle with
perfectionism and self-doubt.

Especially for...

*Name anyone (or situation)
you hold in your heart this day.*

creativity & delight

TUESDAY MORNING

QUIET REFLECTION

creativity & delight

- JOURNAL PROMPT -

*As I ponder this moment and
the day before me...*

What areas of my life would benefit from
a more curious, compassionate, and creative outlook?

TUESDAY MORNING

GOING FORTH

May I remember today that
I am part of an unfolding story…

May I listen with curiosity to
Each plot that thickens,
Each chapter that closes,
Each new adventure that beckons.

May I deepen my awareness of
the presence of mystery.

May I see in every moment
the spark of creation.

May I rejoice in the wonder of
this improbable journey.

creativity & delight

Tuesday Evening

Muses work
all day long
and then at night
get together
and dance.

-EDGAR DEGAS-

TUESDAY EVENING

QUIET CENTERING

Take a couple of slow, deep breaths.

*Enjoy a few moments of quiet to
become present to the gifts of the evening.*

GREETING THE EVENING

*Clouds come floating
into my life
no longer to shed rain
or usher storm
but to give colour to
my sunset sky.*

- RABINDRANATH TAGORE -

TUESDAY EVENING

THANKSGIVINGS

For poets who
continue to speak to us,

For teachers who
continue to show us new paths,

For magicians who
continue to dazzle us,

For musicians who
continue to lift our spirits,

For artists of all kinds who
continue to transform our everyday lives,

I give thanks.

This evening, I am especially grateful for...

Recall the events of the day with gratitude.

TUESDAY EVENING

ENTREATIES

Oh stars in the night sky,
may your shimmering light
shine on me and

All who feel stuck.

All whose creative well has run dry.

All who have lost their child-like imagination.

Especially for...

*Name anyone (or situation)
you hold in your heart this evening.*

creativity & delight

TUESDAY EVENING

QUIET REFLECTION

-JOURNAL PROMPT-

As I take stock of the day,

In what ways have I used my creative gifts?

Where have I seen beauty today?

What has delighted me?

creativity & delight

TUESDAY EVENING

CLOSING THE EVENING

As sunset slips into moonlight
may I heed the words of the philosopher/poet:

Finish each day and be done with it.
You have done what you could.
Some blunders and absurdities have crept in;
Forget them as soon as you can.
Tomorrow is a new day.
You shall begin it serenely and with
too high a spirit to be
encumbered with your old nonsense.

- RALPH WALDO EMERSON -

May it be so.

WEDNESDAY

REST & RENEWAL

Wednesday Morning

We can make our minds
so like still water
that beings gather about us
that they may see,
it may be,
their own images,
and so live for a moment with
a clearer,
perhaps even with
a fiercer life
because of our quiet.

-WILLIAM BUTLER YEATS-

WEDNESDAY MORNING

QUIET CENTERING

"Contemplation is a long, loving look at the real."

-WILLIAM MCNAMARA-

Take a couple of slow, deep breaths.

Enjoy a few moments of quiet to become present to this new day.

GREETING THE DAY

I greet this morning mindful of
the renewable energy
found in restorative rest.
May the gentle breeze and the dappled sky
fill me with peace.
May the gurgling stream and the song of the bird
fill me with the music of all creation.

WEDNESDAY MORNING

THANKSGIVINGS

Thanks be to the Spirit of Renewal
within me and around me
that I have awakened this day to
the awakening of life itself.

For the warmth of the sun,
For life growing from the ground,
For the strong waves of the sea,
For all that is flourishing within me,

I give thanks.

Today, I am especially grateful for...

*As you begin the day give thanks for
what you notice around you and within you.*

WEDNESDAY MORNING

ENTREATIES

May love kindle a flame
within my heart for:

All who are weary and heavy-laden.

All who struggle to experience the
restorative power of rest.

All who feel trapped in
relentless busyness and chaos.

Especially for...

*Name anyone (or situation)
you hold in your heart this day.*

rest & renewal

WEDNESDAY MORNING

QUIET REFLECTION

rest & renewal

- JOURNAL PROMPT -

**As I ponder this moment and
the day before me...**

What areas of my life would benefit from
more rest and renewal?

WEDNESDAY MORNING

GOING FORTH

As I contemplate
the wonders of this new day,
may I take a long, loving look at
the way things are:

Shadow and Light.
Despair and Delight.
Exhaustion and Energy.
Madness and Soundness.
Anxiety and Equanimity.
Doing and Being.

May I be ever mindful of
the rhythms of each day.

May I be patient with
the unfolding seasons.

May it be so.

Wednesday Evening

Rest satisfied with
doing well,
and leave others to
talk of you
as they please.

—PYTHAGORAS—

WEDNESDAY EVENING

QUIET CENTERING

Take a couple of slow, deep breaths.

*Enjoy a few moments of quiet to
become present to the gifts of the evening.*

GREETING THE EVENING

At the close of this day,
may love watch over me this night.

Where there is noise,
let there be places of quiet.

Where there is chaos,
let there be places of peace.

Where there is conflict
let there be places of harmony.

WEDNESDAY EVENING

THANKSGIVINGS

As the sun rests on the horizon,
I give thanks for:

Time to be quiet.

Time to reflect.

Time to kick off my shoes
and take a load off.

This evening, I am especially grateful for…

Recall the events of the day with gratitude.

WEDNESDAY EVENING

ENTREATIES

Oh stars in the night sky,
may your shimmering light
shine on me and

All who are exhausted and spent.

All who keep vigil beside
the bedsides of the dying.

All who hang in limbo.

All who dwell in the liminal space of
neither here nor there.

Especially for...

*Name anyone (or situation)
you hold in your heart this evening.*

rest & renewal

WEDNESDAY EVENING

QUIET REFLECTION

-JOURNAL PROMPT-

As I take stock of the day,

When did I experience opportunities to pause and reflect?

Were there times when *doing nothing* was the best thing?

How will I *unwind* tonight?

rest & renewal

WEDNESDAY EVENING

CLOSING THE EVENING

May the blanket of night
enfold me.

May the shining moon
watch over me.

May the rhythm of the waves
lull me to sleep.

May the steady stars
guide my dreams.

This night.
And always.

May it be so.

THURSDAY

COURAGE & CALLING

Thursday Morning

We shall awaken
from our dullness
and rise vigorously
toward justice.

If we fall in love
with creation
deeper and deeper,
we will respond to
its endangerment
with passion.

—HILDEGARD OF BINGEN—

THURSDAY MORNING

QUIET CENTERING

Take a couple of slow, deep breaths.

Enjoy a few moments of quiet to become present to this new day.

GREETING THE DAY

*I am the flame above
the beauty in the fields;
I shine in the waters;
I burn in the sun, the moon, and the stars.
And with the airy wind,
I quicken all things vitally by
an unseen,
all-sustaining life.*

-HILDEGARD OF BINGEN-

THURSDAY MORNING

THANKSGIVINGS

Thanks be to the Courageous Spirit
within me and around me
that I have awakened this day to
the awakening of life itself.

For the grit and grace to
face a new day,

For an inner voice that
calls forth my best,

For the audacity to believe that
I can make a difference in the world around me,

I give thanks.

Today, I am especially grateful for…

*As you begin the day give thanks for
what you notice around you and within you.*

courage & calling

THURSDAY MORNING

ENTREATIES

May love kindle a flame
within my heart for:

All who hunger for justice.

All who thirst for peace.

All who do not grow weary
caring for the earth and
working for good causes.

Especially for...

*Name anyone (or situation)
you hold in your heart this day.*

courage & caring

THURSDAY MORNING

QUIET REFLECTION

- JOURNAL PROMPT -

As I ponder this moment and the day before me...

How can I use my gifts to make the world around me better?

THURSDAY MORNING

GOING FORTH

Let the beauty we love be what we do.

–RUMI–

May I be present to the duties of the day.

May I not go down too many
rabbit-holes of distraction.

May I not crave to be perfect.

May I hear the courageous call of love
in the work I do, in the words I say,
and in the voices of those I meet
along the way.

May the beauty of what I love
be what I do this day.

May it be so.

courage & calling

Thursday Evening

Life is a hard battle anyway.

If we laugh and sing a little
as we fight the
good fight of freedom,
it makes it all go easier.

I will not allow my life's light
to be determined by
the darkness
around me.

—SOJOURNER TRUTH—

THURSDAY EVENING

QUIET CENTERING

Take a couple of slow, deep breaths.

*Enjoy a few moments of quiet to
become present to the gifts of the evening.*

GREETING THE EVENING

As I settle into the afterglow
and aftermath of the day,
May I not grow weary in care and compassion.
May I find reservoirs of strength that
will sustain me as long as this life endures.

At the closing of this day
may I rest assured that
I have done the best I could
with what I have
at this time.

THURSDAY EVENING

THANKSGIVINGS

For the moon and stars at night,

For the rhythmic waves of the sea,

For all that is tenacious and growing within me,

I give thanks.

As the day dims,

I am especially grateful for…

Recall the events of the day with gratitude.

THURSDAY EVENING

ENTREATIES

Oh stars in the night sky,
may your shimmering light
shine on me
and all who need:

Courage to face the darkness of the night.

Serenity to let go and sink into rest.

Wisdom and energy to respond
to the call of a new day.

Especially for...

*Name anyone (or situation)
you hold in your heart this evening.*

courage & caring

THURSDAY EVENING

QUIET REFLECTION

-JOURNAL PROMPT-

As I take stock of the day,

In what ways have I used my gifts to
make the world around me a better place?

courage & calling

THURSDAY EVENING

CLOSING THE EVENING

May this night bring
the peace of slumber.

May love shine on me
like the stars.

May purpose and meaning
fill my days.

May strength and wisdom
fill my dreams.

This night.
And always.

May it be so.

FRIDAY

HEALING & WHOLENESS

Friday Morning

These pains you feel
are messengers.

Listen to them.

- RUMI -

FRIDAY MORNING

QUIET CENTERING

Take a couple of slow, deep breaths.

Enjoy a few moments of quiet to
become present to this new day.

GREETING THE DAY

For a few moments
may I lay aside any
grief, sorrow, or worry
and notice the beauty
in the world around me:

The mists hovering over the meadows.
The sunlight dancing through the leaves.
The grass poking up through the sidewalk.
The moon peeking through
a blue sky.

FRIDAY MORNING

THANKSGIVINGS

For the healing power of being in nature,

For another day of getting out of bed,

For a heart that beats with love,

For the wound that continues to heal,

For being able to live, move, and have my being,

I give thanks.

Today, I am especially grateful for...

*As you begin the day give thanks for
what you notice around you and within you.*

healing & wholeness

FRIDAY MORNING

ENTREATIES

For the holes in life that will never be whole,
may beauty blossom and grow
around the edges.

May love kindle a flame within my heart for:

All who are suffering and longing for healing.

All who are giving care and longing for a break.

All who are broken and longing for wholeness.

All who are experiencing the fatigue of
shouldering responsibility and toting a heavy load.

Especially for…

*Name anyone (or situation)
you hold in your heart this day.*

healing & wholeness

FRIDAY MORNING

QUIET REFLECTION

healing & wholeness

- JOURNAL PROMPT -

*As I ponder this moment and
the day before me...*

What areas of my life need healing and wholeness?

FRIDAY MORNING

GOING FORTH

I place my hands upon my heart with compassion and care.

May my heart be open.

May my well-being be at ease.

May I be upheld and strengthened with all goodness and grace.

May I know the healing power of love

this day and always.

May it be so.

Friday Evening

I have been
bent and broken,
but
-I hope-
into a better
shape.

– EMILY DICKINSON –

FRIDAY EVENING

QUIET CENTERING

Take a couple of slow, deep breaths.

*Enjoy a few moments of quiet to
become present to the gifts of the evening.*

GREETING THE EVENING

O, Great Mystery of Love:

You are the cause of all movement.
You are the breath of all creatures.
You are the salve that purifies our souls.
You are the ointment that heals our wounds.
You are the fire that warms our hearts.
You are the light that guides our feet.

Let all the world praise you.

-HILDEGARD OF BINGEN-

FRIDAY EVENING

THANKSGIVINGS

For helpers and healers who offer
comfort and encouragement,

For caregivers who give their all,

For family and friends who
check in with us,

For birds, wildlife, and pets that
bring joy and companionship,

I give thanks.

At the dimming of this day,
I am especially grateful for...

Recall the events of the day with gratitude.

healing & wholeness

FRIDAY EVENING

ENTREATIES

Oh stars in the night sky,
may your shimmering light
shine on me and

All those who feel broken.

AND

All those who can't seem to
catch a break.

Especially for...

*Name anyone (or situation)
you hold in your heart this evening.*

healing & wholeness

FRIDAY EVENING

QUIET REFLECTION

-JOURNAL PROMPT-

As I take stock of the day,

Where have I witnessed moments of
healing and wholeness?

What is helping?

healing & wholeness

FRIDAY EVENING

CLOSING THE EVENING

As day collapses into night,

May I find rest.

May I find contentment.

May I find strength.

May I be free of anxiety.

This night.
And always.

May it be so.

SATURDAY

WELCOME & HOSPITALITY

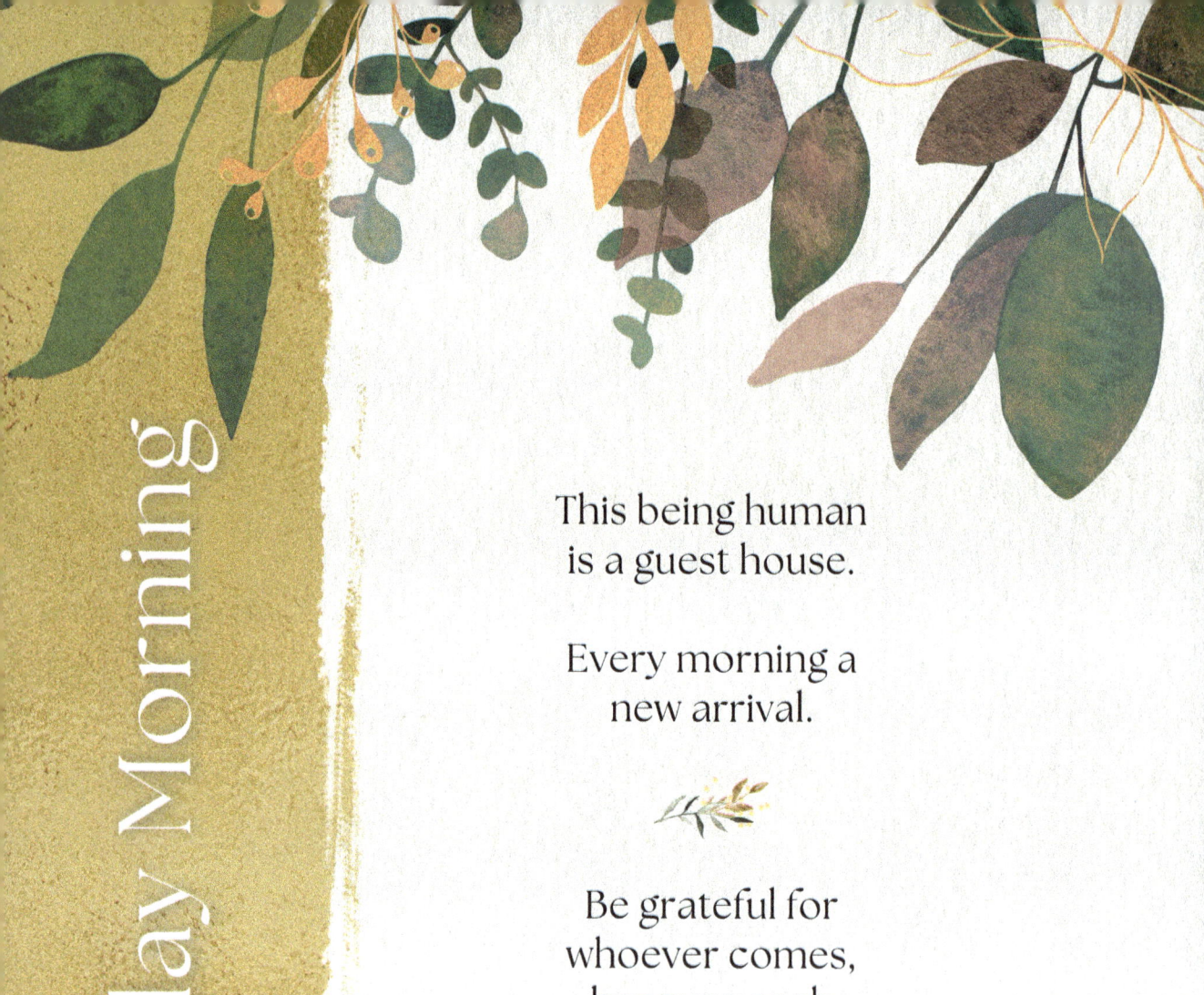

Saturday Morning

This being human
is a guest house.

Every morning a
new arrival.

Be grateful for
whoever comes,
because each
has been sent
as a guide
from beyond.

—RUMI—

SATURDAY MORNING

QUIET CENTERING

Take a couple of slow, deep breaths.

Enjoy a few moments of quiet to become present to this new day.

GREETING THE DAY

*Wake at dawn with a winged heart
and give thanks for another day of loving.*

-KAHIL GIBRAN-

I bless this new day
never known or given before.
May I welcome each hour as a visitor
bearing unknown gifts.
May I see light and love in others' eyes.
May each day of this journey
open my heart to compassion and surprise.

SATURDAY MORNING

THANKSGIVINGS

Thanks be to the Spirit of
Welcome and Hospitality
within me and around me
that I have awakened this day to
the awakening of life itself.

For those who demonstrate care and concern,

For those who welcome the stranger,

For those who remember to say
"please" and *"thank you,"* and *"you're welcome,"*

I give thanks.

Today, I am especially grateful for…

*As you begin the day give thanks for
what you notice around you and within you.*

SATURDAY MORNING

ENTREATIES

May love kindle a flame
within my heart for:

All who are without shelter and safety.

All who are estranged from loved ones.

All who do not feel at home in
body, mind, or spirit.

Especially for...

*Name anyone (or situation)
you hold in your heart this day.*

welcome & hospitality

SATURDAY MORNING

QUIET REFLECTION

- JOURNAL PROMPT -

*As I ponder this moment and
the day before me...*

How can I offer welcome and hospitality,
care and concern to myself and others?

welcome & hospitality

SATURDAY MORNING

GOING FORTH

I have lived long enough to know:

Life is short.

So,

May I endeavor to be kind.

May I recognize the teachers in every encounter.

May I go forth into this day with a welcoming spirit and hospitality in my heart.

May it be so.

Saturday Evening

Not knowing
when the dawn
will come
I open every door.

– EMILY DICKINSON –

SATURDAY EVENING

QUIET CENTERING

Take a couple of slow, deep breaths.

*Enjoy a few moments of quiet to
become present to the gifts of the evening.*

GREETING THE EVENING

I welcome this night with a grateful heart.

May the moon surround me with
light in the darkness.

May peace shine on me
like the stars.

May the slumbering sounds of
the earth sing their lullabies.

SATURDAY EVENING

welcome & hospitality

THANKSGIVINGS

As dusk descends
and the stars begin to appear,

I give thanks for:

Warm places of welcome.

Reconnections and homecomings.

Acts of beauty and kindness.

I am especially grateful for…

Recall the events of the day with gratitude…

SATURDAY EVENING

ENTREATIES

Oh stars in the night sky,
may your shimmering light
shine on all who are

Without a place to call home.

Without a place of welcome.

Without a place of safety and security.

May comfort and belonging
be close this night.

Especially for...

*Name anyone (or situation)
you hold in your heart this evening.*

welcome & hospitality

SATURDAY EVENING

QUIET REFLECTION

-JOURNAL PROMPT-

As I take stock of the day,

How have I experienced welcome and hospitality?

In what ways have I extended
care, concern, and courtesy to others?

welcome & hospitality

SATURDAY EVENING

CLOSING THE EVENING

On my heart and on my house,
The blessing of openness and kindness.

In my coming and in my going,
The peace that baffles understanding.

In my life and on my journey,
The hope of hospitality along the way.

In my endings and new beginnings,
The arms of love to welcome me home.

This night.
And always.

May it be so.

SUNDAY

RITUAL & CELEBRATION

Sunday Morning

Everybody needs
beauty as well as bread.

Places to play in
and pray in,
where nature
may heal
and give strength
to body and soul.

– JOHN MUIR –

SUNDAY MORNING

QUIET CENTERING

Take a couple of slow, deep breaths.

Enjoy a few moments of quiet to become present to this new day.

GREETING THE DAY

Whether walking in nature,
singing songs, or sharing a meal,
May I be open to all that
flows from this day.

So, let the juice of the fruit
run down my chin.
Let wonder wash over me
again and again.
Let the stars rain down and
fill up my bowl.
Let the feast begin,
Let it nourish my soul.

SUNDAY MORNING

THANKSGIVINGS

Thanks be to the Spirit of Life
within me and around me
that I have awakened this day to
the awakening of life itself.

For the sustenance of celebration,
For the power of remembrance,
For the comfort of ritual,

I give thanks.

Today, I am especially grateful for...

*As you begin the day give thanks for
what you notice around you and within you.*

SUNDAY MORNING

ENTREATIES

May love kindle a flame
within my heart for:

All who hunger and thirst for
community and connection.

All who face milestones alone.

All who long for meaning, purpose,
and new beginnings.

Especially for...

*Name anyone (or situation)
you hold in your heart this day.*

ritual & celebration

SUNDAY MORNING

QUIET REFLECTION

- JOURNAL PROMPT -

*As I ponder this moment and
the day before me...*

What rituals remain important to me?

What moments or milestones need commemorating?

ritual & celebration

SUNDAY MORNING

GOING FORTH

Bring your damaged goods to the table.
Lay them on the soft white linens
Smoothed by loving hands.

Hear the words.
Feel the silence.
Receive your bread.
Be warmed by the wine.

The door awaits you.
The bells chime.

-NEVIN COMPTON TRAMMELL-

ritual & celebration

Sunday Evening

Something
opens our wings.

Something
makes boredom and
hurt disappear.

Someone
fills the cup in
front of us:

We taste
only sacredness.

—RUMI—

SUNDAY EVENING

QUIET CENTERING

Take a couple of slow, deep breaths.

*Enjoy a few moments of quiet to
become present to the gifts of the evening.*

GREETING THE EVENING

Blessed be this night.
May I know deep peace
within me and around me:
In the running wave.
In the flowing air.
In the quiet earth.
In the shining stars.

May deep peace sustain me through the night
and bring me safely to a new day.

SUNDAY EVENING

THANKSGIVINGS

As life sifts and settles into the evening,

I give thanks for:

Grace and gladness.

Meaning and mystery.

Good food and health.

Sacred moments and memories.

I am especially grateful for…

Recall the events of the day with gratitude…

SUNDAY EVENING

ENTREATIES

Oh stars in the night sky,
May your shimmering light
shine on me and

All who long for new stories.

All who need something to
look forward to.

All who yearn for some small
transcendence in everyday life.

Especially for...

*Name anyone (or situation)
you hold in your heart this evening.*

ritual & celebration

SUNDAY EVENING

QUIET REFLECTION

ritual & celebration

-JOURNAL PROMPT-

As I take stock of the day,

What rituals have nourished me?

What rituals, if any, need letting go?

In what ways have I
elevated everyday life today?

SUNDAY EVENING

CLOSING THE EVENING

At the close of this day,

May love enfold me this night.

May I rest in the calm of all calm.

May I sleep in the well of all well-being.

May I dream in the peace of all peace.

Now and forever.

May it be so.

CLOSING

THE UNFOLDING STORY

The poet lights the light
and fades away.

But the light
goes on
and on.

-EMILY DICKINSON-

THE UNFOLDING STORY

And so, as our stories continue to unfold,

May we keep listening for
new harmonies emerging from
all the bluster.

May we keep looking for
the poetry hidden in
less-traveled roads.

May we keep embracing new ways to
elevate each day as it comes.

May it all be so.

Thank you for joining me on this quest.

ACKNOWLEDGEMENTS

WITH GRATITUDE

ACKNOWLEDGEMENTS

As with any creative or life endeavor, there are the ongoing tasks of *integration* and *individuation*. That is, being grateful for the influences of the past, incorporating their goodness, and then, finding your own voice and way. This project gave me a unique opportunity to engage in those meaningful tasks.

Being steeped in the language of spirituality, poetry, choral music, and liturgical rituals my whole life, I acknowledge that those rhythms have seeped deeply into my bones. The tenor and cadence of **Each Day As It Comes** springs forth from that well of beauty. This work is also born out of my own personal experience of finding my way through change and absorbing heartbreaking loss. A continuing journey.

I owe abundant gratitude to communities, writers, mentors, and friends who have helped to shape this particular work:

To the Iona Community and the prayers and daily concerns they embody; to the Celtic writer John O'Donohue whose writings continue to buoy me; to the poets Robert Frost, Mary Oliver, and Minton Sparks for influencing and illuminating so many of my developmental stages; to Susan Cain, whose books and Quiet Life Community elevate the often-hidden gifts of introversion and quiet reflection; to Martha W. Hickman, whose book of daily meditations, **Healing After Loss,** is a balm every morning; to Judith Draper who exquisitely holds the stories; to the mountains and art of Asheville and the friends who continue to be present; to Mike and Liz Berger for the magic they bring to life and learning; to John Halbert for nudging me to journal again; to Marjorie Halbert for bringing years of music and liturgy to life. Whenever our creative energies come together, our unmatched synergy creates an indelible "thin place."

When you're finding your way through hard changes and tough losses, the steady patterns of connection and companionship are bright lights shining in the darkness. For Patty, Jenifer, Craig, Bella, Scarlett, Barbara, Jeffrey, Addie, Tony, Sharon, Ellen, George, Matt, Mary Enola, Linda L., Catherine, Linda K., Mignon, LeeAnn, Elizabeth, Katherine, Nev III, extended family, friends, neighbors, hospice staff, therapists, cats, dogs, birds and wildlife, I give a deep, deep bow of thanks. Your presence, support, messages, inclusion, and encouragement make all the difference.

Finally, to Nevin, whose very life was a poem. You continue to inspire me from the other side of the river. Our love story helps me to face each day as it comes. I am grateful beyond words.

I also wish to acknowledge the following voices, both ancient and contemporary, for the poetic wisdom they bring to this book:

HILDEGARD of BINGEN
(1098-1179) German Benedictine abbess, poet, musician, mystic, medical writer, polymath.

RUMI
(1207-1273) Sufi poet.

EMILY DICKINSON
(1830-1886) American poet.

SAPPHO of LESBOS
(c. 630 - c. 570 BC) Greek lyric poet.

LEWIS CARROLL
(1832-1898) English writer, poet, mathematician, photographer.

EDGAR DEGAS
(1837-1917) French Impressionist artist.

RABINDRANATH TAGORE
(1861-1941) Bengali poet, composer, philosopher.

RALPH WALDO EMERSON
(1803-1882) American poet, essayist, abolitionist; Leader of the Transcendentalist Movement.

WILLIAM BUTLER YEATS
(1865-1939) Irish poet, Nobelist.

WILLIAM MCNAMARA ("Abba Willie")
(1926-2015) Contemplative Carmelite monk.

PYTHAGORAS of SAMOS
(c. 570-c. 495 BC) Greek philosopher, polymath.

SOJOURNER TRUTH (Isabella Baumfree)
(1797-1883) African American abolitionist and activist for civil rights and women's rights.

KAHLIL GIBRAN
(1883-1931) Lebanese American writer, poet, and visual artist.

JOHN MUIR
(1838-1914) Scottish American author, naturalist, and environmental philosopher.

NEVIN COMPTON TRAMMELL
(1937-2023) American poet.

ABOUT THE AUTHOR | DESIGNER

Karen Lee Turner is an artist, educator and retreat leader. She holds a master's degree in counseling and a doctorate in educational leadership from Vanderbilt University's Peabody College of Education and Human Development.

Her essays have been published in the award-winning spiritual life journal, *Weavings*, as well as *Leading from Within: Poetry that Sustains the Courage to Lead*. She is a Lilly Endowment grant awardee for her work as a liturgical musician.

She writes, paints, and designs retreats and courses in her colorful, light-filled studio just outside of Nashville where she is assisted by her two Maine Coon cats.

karenleeturner.com

SWOON RIVER PRESS is the independent
publisher of books, journals, courses, and
other creative works by artist and author
Karen Lee Turner and
posthumously the works of the poet
Nevin Compton Trammell.

swoonriverpress.com

www.ingramcontent.com/pod-product-compliance
Lightning Source LLC
Chambersburg PA
CBHW061357010526
44107CB00012B/960